BUSY DADDY!

BY NUWAN SIRIWARNASINGHE

Illustrations By
Rania Tulba

"Good morning, Daddy!"
He is feeling sleepy and snuggly,
and tosses and turns in his cozy bed.
"Come on, Daddy, it's time to get up!
The sun is shining!"

**Getting up early means you have time to
eat breakfast, brush your teeth and put on
your clothes for the fun day ahead!**

BREAKFAST DADDY

Daddy loves his porridge!
With some berries and fruit galore.
He sometimes adds honey
or nuts, and goes,
"Crunch, crunch, munch, munch, munch!"
He shares his breakfast with me.

**A good breakfast gives you energy
and helps you grow.**

READY DADDY!

Daddy gets ready.
Pants, socks, shirt, trousers.
He tidies his hair, then it's time to go.
"Oh, don't forget your shoes, Daddy!"
He gives me a cuddle and says,
"I'm ready for the day!"

Always dress well wherever you go.

PARK, DADDY!

Daddy takes me to the park.
Oh, I feel the nice fresh air
and listen to the birds sing.
The park is where you'll find Daddy and
me running, jumping, and swinging.
We love to be active and strong.
We laugh and smile all day!

**Going to the park is great way
to keep Daddy healthy.**

SHOPPING DADDY!

Daddy and I look at all the pretty clothes
and smell the perfume at the shops.
We listen to all the noise:
Beep! Ding! Boop!
We go to the supermarket too.
Is Daddy buying some yummy food for me?
Shopping with Daddy is fun.

**When out and about be sure
to always hold your daddy's hand.
He will guide you, protect you
and show you the way.**

SAD DADDY!

Sometimes Daddy is sad.
His smile is upside down,
which makes me feel sorry for him.
I bring him his favourite snack.
But it's my hugs and playing with me
that really makes him smile.
I love to cheer him up
because he's the best daddy ever.
"It's okay to be sad, Daddy."

**When you are feeling blue,
remember what makes you happy.**

I love it when Daddy comes home.
He opens the door wide, and says,
"I'm home!"
I run to hug him,
and he hugs me back really tight
because we've missed each other.
We play games and have dinner together.
Home is where Daddy belongs,
with me and the family!

Daddys need to go out of the house but they always come home to us. Being together and being apart is a part of family life.

I ♥
Cooking

BUSY DADDY!

Wow! Daddy is really busy!
He is talking on the phone,
typing on the computer,
and trying to cook lunch.
"You can't juggle everything at once
– you're not a clown!"
"Watch out, Daddy!"
I help my daddy by telling him to do
one thing before starting another.

**It's important to finish one thing at a time
and do each thing as best as we can.**

Oh, poor Daddy.
He had such a long day.
He worked so hard and did his best and
now he needs to put his feet up.
But he left his stinky socks on the floor!
I tell him they smell so bad,
and he should pick up after himself!

**You must help keep the house clean
by tidying up.
Always put away your toys and books,
and don't forget your stinky socks!**

SURPRISED DADDY!

Daddy is enjoying watching TV.
I pop out from behind the chair:
"Peek-a-boo!" I shout out loud.
Daddy jumps in the air!
"Yikes! You surprised me!" he cries out.
He laughs and hugs me tight.

Sometimes we can surprise people by hiding and popping out. This can be a fun game, but we should also be careful not to scare them too much.

GRUMPY DADDY!

Sometimes Daddy gets in a bad mood
- he grumps, snorts,
and "hmmphs" like a dragon!
"Oh, Daddy, you cannot eat ice cream for
breakfast, lunch, and dinner
because you are in a bad mood!"
"It's not good for your tummy or teeth!"

**It's not good to have too much of anything,
or it will make you sick or spoil your fun.
A balance of everything is the best way.**

CRYING DADDY!

Daddy is in the garden,
running around the pond.
But he slips,
Splash!
Oh no!
"There, there," I say to Daddy.
I tell him it's okay to cry
if he has a boo, boo!
I give him a hug and a band-aid,
and he's all better to try again.

**It's okay to make mistakes, and it's
important to try again and keep learning.**

STORY TIME

SICK DADDY!

Daddy has a dripping nose
and he sneezes and coughs.
"Achoo!"
Oh, dear, he's got the sniffles!
He needs some tissues and some cuddles.
"I'll read you a story
and make you some soup."
"Don't worry, Daddy, I'll look after you."

**It's important to drink water, rest in bed
and take your medicine when you are not well.
And have lots of cuddles, too!**

HUNGRY DADDY!

Daddy is hungry!
Roar! Grumble!
Is Daddy's stomach making music?
He needs some food to fill his tummy
– it must be dinner time!
Let's go to the kitchen and see
what we can cook.
Carrots, broccoli, peas, and beans.
Only the yummiest vegetables, please!

**Tasty vegetables make you healthy and
strong and stop the tummy-rumbles.**

SILLY DADDY!

Daddy sometimes makes goofy faces and
funny noises: "Hooooonk! Brrraaapp!"
He puts broccoli on his head!
"Oh, silly Daddy!" I cheer happily.
"But food is for your tummy,
not for your hair.
Silly games come after broccoli!"
He scoops me high in the air,
"You're right, my little munchkin!"

There is a time and a place for fun.
You can be silly and playful
when you have finished eating.

WC

POTTY TIME DADDY!

Oh! What's that smell?
"Is it time for the bathroom, Daddy?"
"Come on, let's go use the potty, and
don't be shy, it's a normal thing
we all do!"
Everyone needs to use the potty.

**So, when you feel a tummy rumble
or a pressure down below, go for a wee-wee
or a poo-poo.**

SLEEPY DADDY!

Yawwwwwn!
The bedtime story Daddy was reading to
me has put him to sleep!
I stroke his hair, tuck him in his blanket
and whisper, "Good night, Daddy."
I kiss his forehead and turn off the light.
"Thank you, Daddy,
for all that you do for me.
You're my hero, my friend,
my very own Daddy."

When you're sleepy, don't fight it;
your body needs to rest, and snuggle!

I LOVE YOU DADDY!

BUSY DADDY!

Copyright © 2024 by Nuwan Siriwarnasinghe

All Rights Reserved
No part of this book may be reproduced in any form, by photocopying or by any electronic or mechanical means, including information storage or retrieval systems, without permission in writing from both the copyright owner and the publisher of this book.

ISBN 978-2-6828-6194-0
First Published Date by 2024

www.ingramcontent.com/pod-product-compliance
Lightning Source LLC
LaVergne TN
LVHW071656180726
843512LV00002B/462